Resilience

Re-sil-ience : \ri-ˈzil-yən(t)s\ **1:** the capability of a strained body to recover its size and shape after deformation caused especially by compressive stress **2:** an ability to recover from or adjust easily to misfortune or change (Merriam-Webster).

April Frances Federico

To order additional copies of this book, contact:
Xlibris
844-714-8691
www.Xlibris.com
Orders@Xlibris.com

ISBN:	Softcover	978-1-6641-4158-2
	EBook	978-1-6641-4157-5

Print information available on the last page

Rev. date: 11/05/2020

Contents

POEMS:

Acknowledgements

THANK YOU to Professor Renee Soto for helping me find my voice in poetry and THANK YOU to Tiana Clark who told me I have a gift for writing and writing poetry.

To the two most influential women in
my life: my mom, and Grammy.

"Wasn't there one girl who made a paint brush out her own hair?"

I plop down onto my wooden chair—
it's been a long day, but this is what I've been

looking forward to. My poor back bends over
for the umpteenth time to pull out my sketchbook—also made of wood,
but has been morphed to convert to the shape of my binders.

I rip a page out of it, as if I'm angry,
but I shouldn't take that single piece of canvas

paper for granted. We all suffered a death one way
or another. The other artists just paint random things on a canvas as if they
don't mean anything. They say an artist's work is better interpreted

after their death. My life is the tree that
has been cut down, only to have the flowers' seeds

tell my story over and over again, but in different forms. Life is a work of art and we're all just living it
the way we would, ideally, like it to be portrayed.

The day I met my best friend, Katelyn

I am thrown overboard after graduating high school. I tread water—refusing to drown-- until a magic carpet of a raft comes to me. I sleep anxiously for fifty-four nights, knowing I'm about to embark on an important voyage in two months, hoping I'm in the right direction, until something clinks upon my raft—a message in a bottle. I pull out the rolled up parchment paper without struggle. In indistinct letters it reads, *Come to me, April— Katelyn.* I look up to blue lights coming out of a figure's eyes in the distance. It's another girl oaring her way towards my direction and my raft pulls me towards her canoe. I'm face-to-face with a brunette, big-eyed, girl in a red dress as she says, "you don't know this, yet, but we're going to be best friends." And the last scene of "Breakfast at Tiffany's" takes the sky's place.

April and October

My name is April, but my evil twin is
October – a very vicious month. She is known to those who have not
quite gotten to completely know me— we are both in one body.
Currently, I am April–
a girl who has seen struggle firsthand,
and prays that no one else goes through
what I have experienced in twenty-two years.
When I'm around other people, I exude a
warm, pleasant, comforting breeze, and you can
always smell those sweet scents of fruit and vanilla.
She has a smile that illuminates, even in the darkest
of rooms, and walks as if I have wings and a halo.
Then there is October— hi! a   complete maniac. She's comical, noisier, crazy, and vulgar. But she just wants to
have fun. She is like an empty April— she is a ghost—white and basic. She can be frightening, sometimes and
unpredictable. She emits a cold breeze. And if you smell directly from the smoke, your nose will burn severely.

You may feel the softness of April, or the roughness of October, and savor the sweetness of April or the pumpkin
spices of October. It doesn't matter because we are the same person, therefore, we have the same feelings. I try
to run away from October because I don't want the "party girl" reputation. It is a pity that some are too blinded
by my failures to see the lover, the compassionate, the caring, the only April you may ever meet.

Punching Bag

"Harder, I know you
can hit harder than
that!" my personal trai-
ner says to me.
I look at her hands,

I look at mine. Hers
are daintier and
tanner, with perfect-
ly manicured, beige
fingernails. I wond-

der about the lines
on your palm and the
even more-detailed
swirls on your fingers.
It's a wonder, all

on its own, where these
elegant, yet vi-
cious parts of our bo-
dies have been. We use
these hands every day,

we just don't realize
it. Touch speaks louder
than our mouths. Our mouths
can't handle the weight
of our words, thus, we ask

our hands to express
them for us. Rather
than swearing at my-
self in the mirror,
I use my hands to

beat myself up, in-
stead, like ivory
mallets beating on
my poor head until
I see purple light.

A Bland Salsa

A slow song comes on, and, conveniently, it's 'it will rain' by Bruno Mars.
I wrap my arms around your neck, just like I would've done to him,
but instead of a spark, sadness and want overcome me.
You don't speak to me, until you say, "spin," and I can somewhat feel the magic of my light pink, bejeweled dress twirling. At least I got something out of that dress.
But still I have a sour taste in my mouth. We're pushed closer together,
and the sourness turns into a choking coarseness. I can't say what a horrible night I'm having,
because then I'd hate myself more for saying I still love you. I still think about what a perfect tango we could've shared together. It could've turned this boredom into absolute spiciness.

The Royal Mermaid

The merlitary-soldiers draw up their swords, the Aquatic Choir sings opera, and Merghan thinks to herself, *time for my life to change.* Gracefully and slowly she swims up to the embellished altar, face-to-face with her future: Prince Adamaris who whispers, "you look amazing, I am so lucky." The opera and vows continue for what seem like hours until they seal their eternal love with a kiss. As she swims down the isle, she repeats to herself, *swim, inhale, blink, swim, exhale, blink, don't look too obvious that you're going to regret this and despise the crab cake and the plethora of coral-candied bread.* As they make their debut to the public of Fishington, she knows she must share her husband with all the oceans and to make the marriage look flawless, even when she also knows she is forced to new rules: no more scandals and practically no time to see her family and friends, only the artiso-mers and other royals—solely duty to her role as Duchess of Amberly. The only people she fears most is King Trident and Poseidon. Fourteen days later and she is cloaked in a dress made of aquamarine scales and a heavy crown of sapphire jewels, pouring in private over mer-memes of old pictures of her—some not so kind. *This is my new life.*

Perfection is a weakness of mine

To be honest, when I was in high school, I strived for perfection and I'll be honest it gave me a little OCD!

I'm trying to gnaw on this idea of being perfect;
I chew it down right to that savory bone marrow
until there's nothing left to even suck on anymore—
at this point all I'm doing is sucking on that
circular piece of bone. The bone is in my right thumb
and I've sucked on it so much to feel like I've lost
all feeling.

Perfection is like sucking on a piece of bone marrow—
you cleanse it of all the meat and the cells that go with it,
until there's nothing anymore. It becomes addictive,
like a fidget toy. People tell you you're doing great by
cleaning it and getting all the necessary juice to make you
feel manly, accomplished, whatever. Then you become
addicted to being perfect and receiving that praise.

Paradise Lost me, but I know it'll find me again

Sitting in Ms. Crane's eleventh grade
British Literature class, my world, and
John Milton world were hanging by a chain,
as he was suffering the loss of his second wife,
and his infant daughter.

Milton counted twelve parts to his whole biblical story,
as I counted mine throughout the years.

1: the year I survived since birth
2: the year I suffered abuse from my babysitter
3: the year I swore for the first time in Washington D.C.
4: the year I do not remember, but remember those of my cousins'
5: the year I started preschool
6: the year I started kindergarten
7: the year I knew what it was like to drift apart from my best friends
8: the year I became familiar with the word, "popularity"
9: the year I knew what it was like to be alone and friendless
10: the year I was convinced that having a best friend and laughing were unacceptable
11: the year I had my first real crush on a boy
12: the year I knew what it was like to be an ostensible middle school "loser."

As I counted the years with the months,
I knew that I would live even after the twelfth
Month,
Year,
Grade,
And far beyond.

John Milton, if you could live after you published your twelfth book,
I could live a long life, too.

My first trip without my mother

Emerging from the dark tunnel underneath the city
of lights. The Parisian sun greets me as I say, "I'm going
to cry from happiness," the sun says, "welcome to a
whole new world, where you are on your own."
The sun blazes my skin, I see in a few pictures,
it's smothering me with kisses.

At around five o'clock the sun turns to twilight, but the
city is already prepared to guide us through the streets
so I don't get lost. The string lights hanging from awnings
and lamp posts luminate the streets as I tell a friend,
"I want to live here one day."

I am still illuminated with joy, for I am home.
Paris had welcomed me with open arms,
just like my mother would have.

A withered sarcophagus at the MET

November 2015, I'm with my then-boyfriend
who seems to be more interested in this girl,
not me or any of the paintings I point out to him,
that I know impressively from studying them in high school.
This girl is like a Cleopatra majoring in history,
just like him and his Marc Antony, and that's how he makes their connection—
she and her short skirt and fur-lined jacket.
I promised myself I wouldn't be jealous, but even she can
tell that I'm pissed—
that he's so focused on their ostensible friendship, than his current affair with me.
Maybe I'm that slave that Marc Antony has an affair with,
Slaving away my time,
Energy,
And my own worth
Only to be recognized in the MET as a withered sarcophagus.

Miracle of even a Single Pentacle

Water slips through my fingers
like a broken promise
for a while I started to let go
of all the things I know.
I began begging for money
like a beggar on the street.
Two days later, I decided to say a prayer
and I was brought a miracle.

It is when you start to feel lost,
when you receive a tarot reading,
and the Ace of Pentacles is drawn.
Just one.
And my fountain has one coin towards my future.

Life is a Masterpiece

I edit.

I'm an editor.
I edit things frequently and I edit things
Ruthlessly.
Every piece of writing is a masterpiece, after all.

I edit.

I'm an editor.
That means nothing is ever good enough for me.
I'm constantly editing my own life—
Writing, erasing, writing, erasing
And sometimes getting a second or third or fourth
Opinion
And making a big jump in your story's plot
Just to fit in your dreams
I guess that's the price you pay for following them.
Life is a masterpiece, after all.

I'm back on Saint Anselm's Campus

to visit my best friend, Katelyn, at my former alma mater—
I haven't been to New Hampshire in well over a year,
because I am always reminded of the time

my black, suede, wedged boots struggled on the ice,
just like I was struggling to stay sane, but I don't fall.

This time, I put on those same black, suede, wedged boots
to go out on the town of Manchester. This time, I am old
enough to order a margarita with Patrón at McGarvey's
instead of chocolate chip cookie dough ice cream at Ben and Jerry's—
and so I walk past that Ben and Jerry's and beeline it to the bar
and order that Margarita with as much Patrón to make me tipsy—
a new high.

This time, I stand with my head held higher as I see no ice
perturbing my strides—the confident *click clack click* as the wedges
of my boots hit the pavement of 100 Saint Anselm Drive.

11:11 a.m. on 11/11/18, 24 hours and 25 minutes after I call it off

I wish you could see yourself and how furious I am,
the pain you've caused,
but I know I am better off without
the aggravation of your absence,
you being a vague flake,
as this supposed relationship is melting without melee
no matter how hard *I* fight for it
even though you said you would stand by me,
even when you were looking for something serious, and I—
I was at my lowest temperament and *we* were living in the shortest days.
It might as well be the first day of winter. Do I dare wait
until the vernal equinox appears?
For you? To see the stars again?
Well, it's 11:11 a.m. the next day, and I already wished to forget about you.

Take Advantage of an Upcoming Opportunity

I walk confidently through the streets of my small town,
sipping a hot cocoa, taking a glance at the purple-lighted Christmas Tree,
and suddenly I feel melancholy—December 3rd is coming up—

six years later and I still dread the date we made our budding love
official, except this time, there are no empty promises under the tree,
like an eager child I opened in a rush, only to find the gift

completely shattered.

I make a beeline six blocks to a Chinese restaurant where the
plates and napkins are set up—just like our first date.
I am alone in the venue, but my mind replays your figure

in your hoodie, gray Converse, and faded Levi's.
I ask for the red wine, this time. *Fuck it,* I say,
I'm going to order the Kung Pow Pork—chow it
down like I've tasted it for the first time!

When I receive the check with two fortune cookies,
I only pay for the meal, and leave the cookies behind
with confidence in knowing what my future holds—

without you.

Beantown: Friday, September 28, 2018

"This is our fucking city." – David Ortiz

I haven't been to Boston in five-hundred-something days;
The automatic voice calls out "Mansfield," "Westwood,"

and just by the familiarity of those towns from the way
my dad and I used to take the train into Boston,

I know we're close. I know we're even closer when
I see the famous Rainbow Swash going through Dorchester;

Orange for the time I was supposed to go into Boston for
New Year's Eve with my sophomore year lover,

Gold for the time I didn't receive a medallion
for being at least in the top ten of my high school class,

Red for the first time I ever had to wear a formal gown—
Junior prom—the evening my classmates tried to ruin for me,

Blue for the countless amounts of ribbons
I didn't win at any track meet I've ever competed in,

Green for the plethora of capers with Chicken Piccatta
ordered in the North End while embracing my Italian heritage,

and Purple for the all of the lights at La Sallette—
when my college boyfriend was texting the whole time.

Despite all the bad things and misfortunes that occurred in
Massachusetts, this is home. This is my fucking city.

Victoria's Secret Love Spell

I google "what will make a guy like you?"
I look up to my top shelf to see the purple
bottle shaped perfectly like a woman's body,
I find my answer right there. I have thirteen
minutes to hose myself down with the love spell—
twice on the neck, once on my left wrist, and
twice much, much lower. I like to say I steal this
secret from Victoria, because I use this trick on
every date.

Just one spritz of fruity perfume has the power to make
any male say, "wow, don't ever change." By the end of the
night, I don't say a word, just my borrowed scent do the talking.

Nothing is more bitter

than black coffee,
especially when it isn't "fresh"—
it came out of the microwave.

I tried to add Splenda to make it sweeter,
but it's just not the same as it once was
when it was young and fresh out of the pot

just like the day we met.

Anyway, I take a sip of my radiated cup of disappointment,
but I settle for it, knowing there is not much I can do.

I keep expecting it to be sweeter by the end of the cup's hoorah,
until the grainy, vile taste of grinds reach by tongue,

and I say, no, I can't do this anymore.

Radiation isn't good for the body, anyway.

Silver Lining

"She was devoted to the moon. In its darkness she found comfort. In its light she found hope." - *Unknown*

I wrote my own *Silver Lining's Playbook*, recently. But gold
is one of my lucky colors.
And I am a firm believer that everything I attempt
will turn from a rusty copper to a sterling silver
to a golden trophy that I win in the end of it all.
I am also a firm believer that there is always
light at the end of the tunnel. Light has always been a motif in my life.

The bleakness of the sciences of Biology and Chemistry
became the adrenaline of Creative Writing and English.

Pas de Chat

Right foot transitions to the left, and I think I'm high off the ground
in the ambience of my performance.
Am I dancing to the orchestra of my life?

Or for our relationship?

I may as well paint the picture of the diamond I had in mind
with my own legs, it's in my repertoire, now.

It always has been.

I master my own leap from stage right to stage left and there I am,
on my side of my own reality.

Relationships needn't be a pas de chat.

Black Lace

Five years pass and I'm mature—
more mature than the girl who would hose herself down
on Victoria's Secret Love Spell.
I take that new, clear bottle filled with that perfect burnt sienna liquid
to my wrist, and my skin doesn't reek
of fruit, but an intoxicating aroma
of self-empowerment.
That girl didn't need a borrowed scent
to bloom into what she is—five years later.

Pot Au Feu

Slowly savoring the moment of each single step
I take downstairs to dine with my mother.
It only took the color red to make me feel like I have returned,

Have you ever had the first sentence of a poem?
Then your mind is on fire, like a pot on the stove for the last line?

That only means that night was a dream that wasn't a dream, at all—
but pure bliss that makes you melt for days, maybe even months later.

ART WORKS

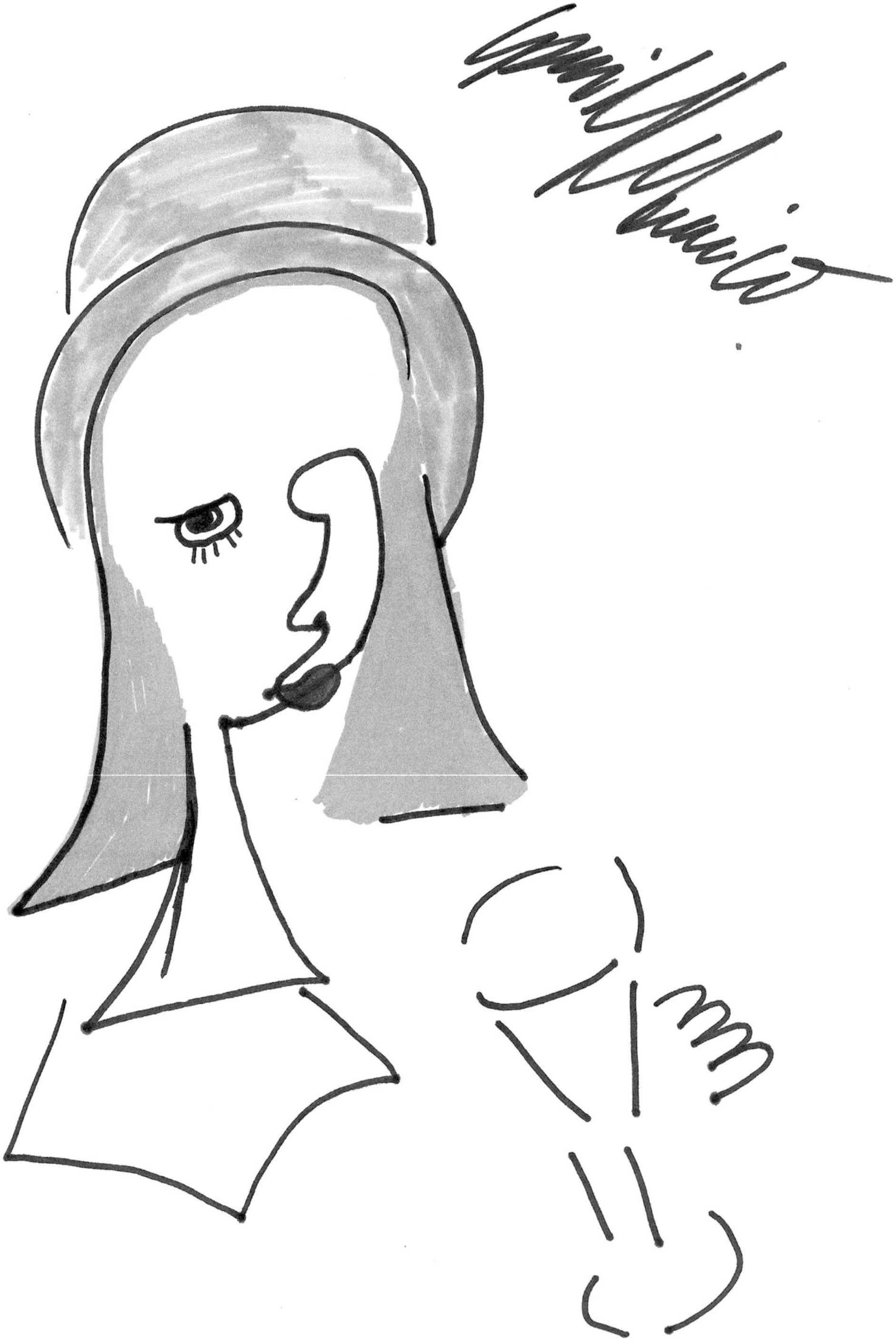

Printed in the United States
By Bookmasters